CONGRESS

BY GEOFFREY M. HORN

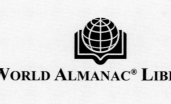

WORLD ALMANAC® LIBRARY

Please visit our web site at: www.worldalmanaclibrary.com
For a free color catalog describing World Almanac® Library's list
of high-quality books and multimedia programs, call 1-800-848-2928 (USA)
or 1-800-387-3178 (Canada). World Almanac® Library's fax: (414) 332-3567.

Library of Congress Cataloging-in-Publication Data

Horn, Geoffrey M.
      The Congress / by Geoffrey M. Horn.
           p. cm. — (World Almanac Library of American government)
      Includes bibliographical references and index.
      ISBN 0-8368-5457-8 (lib. bdg.)
      ISBN 0-8368-5462-4 (softcover)
      1. United States. Congress—Juvenile literature. [1. United States. Congress.] I. Title. II. Series.
      JK1025.H67 2003
      328.73—dc21   2002514111

First published in 2003 by
World Almanac® Library
330 West Olive Street, Suite 100
Milwaukee, WI 53212 USA

Copyright © 2003 by World Almanac® Library.

Project editor: Alan Wachtel
Project manager: Jonny Brown
Cover design and layout: Melissa Valuch
Photo research: Brian Boerner
Indexer: Mary Brod
Production: Jessica L. Yanke

Photo credits: © AP/Wide World Photos: 4 bottom, 10, 11, 12 top, 14, 15 top, 17 bottom, 19 both, 20 both, 21, 22, 23 both, 24, 25 bottom, 27, 28, 30, 31 bottom, 32 top, 33, 34, 37, 38, 39; © Bettmann/CORBIS: 25 top, 32 bottom, 35 top; © CORBIS: 5 top; © EyeWire: 12 bottom, 31 top; Courtesy Library of Congress: 5 bottom, 6, 7, 8, 9, 13, 26 bottom, 35 bottom, 36; National Archives and Records Administration: cover (background), title page, 29; © Reuters NewMedia Inc./CORBIS: 15 bottom, 17 top; Courtesy United States Department of Agriculture photo by Ken Hammond: cover (main), 4 top; Melissa Valuch/© Gareth Stevens, Inc., 2003: 18, 26 top

Printed in the United States of America

1 2 3 4 5 6 7 8 9 07 06 05 04 03

About the Author

GEOFFREY M. HORN is a freelance writer and editor with a lifelong interest in politics and the arts. He is the author of books for young people and adults and has contributed hundreds of articles to encyclopedias and other reference books, including *The World Almanac.* He lives in southwestern Virginia, in the foothills of the Blue Ridge Mountains, with his wife, five cats, and one rambunctious collie. He dedicates this book to Amelia Jane Davidson and her loving parents and grandparents.

TABLE OF CONTENTS

Words that appear in the glossary are printed in **boldface** type the first time they occur in the text.

Chapter One

CONGRESS AND THE CAPITOL

▲ U.S. Capitol, Washington, D.C.

▼ Before he became U.S. president in 1974, Gerald Ford (left) spent more than eight years as Republican leader in the House.

At the center of Washington, D.C., stands the United States Capitol, the great domed building that is home to the Congress of the United States. About sixteen city blocks divide the Capitol from the White House, which is located northwest of the Capitol at 1600 Pennsylvania Avenue.

In the White House sits the president of the United States, chosen every four years in an election in which more than 100 million people cast their ballots. The president heads the **executive branch** of government. In the Capitol sit the 535 members of Congress, which is divided into the Senate and the House of Representatives. The Senate consists of 100 members, two from each of the 50 states. The House is made up of 435 members, elected from 435 separate districts. Congress is the core of the U.S. government's **legislative branch**.

Although the Capitol and the White House are physically close, Congress and the president are separated by more than two hundred years of history and tradition. The executive branch and the legislative branch keep watchful eyes on each other, making sure that neither becomes too powerful. And the courts, or the **judicial branch**, keep a careful watch on them both.

Worthy to Be Remembered

One of the greatest of all members of Congress was Daniel Webster. During the first half of the nineteenth century, he served both in the House of Representatives and in the Senate. These words of his are displayed in the House Chamber:

Let us develop the resources of our land, call forth its powers, build up its institutions, promote all its great interests and see whether we also in our day and generation may not perform something worthy to be remembered.

▶ **Daniel Webster was renowned for his speechmaking.**

THE SEARCH FOR A HOME

America had a congress before it had a president or a **constitution**. The First Continental Congress met in Philadelphia in 1774, two years before the nation declared itself independent from Great Britain. During the 1770s and 1780s, sessions of Congress were also held in Lancaster and York, Pennsylvania; Princeton and Trenton, New Jersey; and Baltimore and Annapolis, Maryland.

▼ **New York's Federal Hall, where Congress met during 1789–90.**

After the Constitution of the United States took effect in March 1789, Congress began meeting at Federal Hall in New York City. On April 30, in the same location, George Washington was sworn in as the first president of the United States. A law passed in 1790 provided that Congress would meet in Philadelphia for the next ten years. During that period, a permanent home for Congress would be built in the new national capital.

★ L'Enfant's design for a national capital was based on a survey map prepared by Andrew Ellicott and Benjamin Banneker. The son of a freed slave, Banneker had little formal education but became well known as an astronomer.

Pierre Charles L'Enfant, the French-born engineer and architect who planned the U.S. capital, chose to place Congress at one of the highest points in the district. He picked a site called Jenkins' Hill, which is now known as Capitol Hill. The cornerstone for the Capitol building was laid on September 18, 1793.

When Congress moved into its new home on November 17, 1800, Washington, D.C., looked very different than it does today. Most of the district was a muddy swamp. The roof of the House leaked, and the Senate ceiling caved in. Many improvements were made during the next thirteen years. However, on August 24, 1814, British troops invaded Washington and set fire to the Capitol. The building would have been completely destroyed if not for a sudden rainstorm.

A WALKING TOUR OF CAPITOL HILL

Capitol Hill is a huge area, including lawns and gardens, a half-dozen congressional office buildings, and the

Words to the Wise

Two words that are easy to confuse are *capital* and *Capitol*. The word *capital* (usually spelled with a small *c*) means a city that serves as a seat of government. For example, Washington, D.C., is the capital of the United States, and Austin is the state capital of Texas. The *Capitol* (spelled with a large *c*) is the building where Congress meets. When spelled with a small *c*, the word *capitol* means the building that houses the legislative branch of a state government. All these words come from the Latin word for "head."

The Capitol Dome

The original plan for the Capitol building was drawn up in 1792 by Dr. William Thornton, who was born in the West Indies. His plan called for a building that would have two wings—one for the Senate, the other for the House. Joining them would be a large circular room, or rotunda, topped by a low dome. Work on the Capitol Rotunda did not start until 1818. The dome, made of wood covered with copper, was finished six years later.

By the 1850s, the Capitol had outgrown its dome. The House and Senate buildings had become much larger, making the dome seem too small. The wooden frame beneath the copper was also a fire hazard. A plan for a much larger dome, made of iron, was approved in 1855, and the interior was completed in 1866.

Atop the dome, facing east, is a female figure—the Statue of Freedom. The height of the Capitol from the base of the East Front entrance to the top of the statue is 288 feet (88 meters). The dome is not the highest point in Washington: that honor belongs to the Washington Monument, which is about 555 feet (169 m) high and was completed in 1885. By law, however, no new building in Washington may be taller than the Capitol.

🔺 **This 1836 view of the Capitol shows a dome much smaller than today's.**

Library of Congress. (See Chapter 4.) At the center of all this is the Capitol building, consisting of five levels and more than five hundred rooms. Below ground, subways and tunnels convey the members of Congress and their staffs from their offices to the Capitol and back again.

The main entrance to the Capitol is the East Front, which faces the U.S. Supreme Court. As you stand at the East Front, the Rotunda is ahead of you, and the dome looms high overhead. To your left is the south wing of the Capitol, where the House of Representatives meets. To your right is the north wing, where the Senate gathers. The legislative chambers are on the second floor.

On the third floor are the entrances to the House and Senate galleries, where you can view the speeches and debates when Congress is in session.

The entrance to the Rotunda is on the second floor. This magnificent room measures 180 feet (55 m) high and 96 feet (29 m) across and is decorated with scenes from United States history. Directly above you as you stand at the center of the Rotunda is the great dome's inner wall. At the uppermost point, or apex, of the dome you can see a painting by the Italian-born artist Constantino Brumidi, which shows George Washington rising up to heaven. Among the Rotunda's many other paintings and statues is a recent addition: a tribute to Lucretia Mott, Elizabeth Cady Stanton, and Susan B. Anthony, three pioneers of the women's rights movement.

▲ Members of the House of Representatives have been meeting in this chamber since 1857.

Making the Capitol Safer

Not all visitors to the Capitol have been peaceful. In 1954, for example, several members of a group seeking independence for Puerto Rico fired guns from the visitors' gallery; five House members were wounded. Another shooting, in 1998, resulted in the deaths of two Capitol police officers. Recent attacks by terrorists against the United States have increased worries about Capitol security.

Construction of a new Capitol Visitor Center has already begun. The center, which is expected to open in 2005, will be located on three underground levels at the East Front of the Capitol. The center will include space for exhibits, video presentations, food services, gift shops, and improved security checkpoints.

WHAT THE CONSTITUTION SAYS

When the **framers** of the Constitution met in Philadelphia in 1787, they faced a difficult problem. Some of the framers came from states with large populations, like Virginia and Pennsylvania. Others came from states with small populations, such as New Jersey and Delaware. The large states favored a Congress in which they would have more seats. Some of the small states wanted a Congress in which every state, no matter how small, would have the same number of seats—and thus the same number of votes.

▼ In this 1940 painting, now displayed at the Capitol, Howard Chandler Christy portrayed the signing of the Constitution. Among the signers was George Washington, shown standing at right.

The framers settled this dispute with a compromise. They established a bicameral Congress—a Congress with two chambers. The number of seats in one chamber, the House of Representatives, is based on population.

Terms and Sessions

Each Congress has a number. The 1st Congress is the one that began meeting in 1789, while the 107th Congress began in January 2001, and the 108th Congress is the one beginning in January 2003. This numbering system is based on the fact that every seat in the House of Representatives comes up for election every two years.

Each Congress is divided into two regular sessions. The first regular session always begins in an odd-numbered year; it starts in January, when the members are sworn in. The second regular session always begins in January of the following year and lasts until the House members' terms expire.

Each state has at least one representative in the House, but the states with the most people get the most seats and, therefore, the most votes. The other chamber, the Senate, is designed to give each state an equal voice. Every state, no matter how large or small, has exactly two senators.

QUALIFICATIONS, TERMS, AND SALARIES

The Constitution describes the qualifications required of members of Congress and sets the lengths of their terms. Article I, Section 2 of the Constitution says that a member of the House of Representatives must be at least twenty-five years old and must have been a citizen of the United States for at least seven years. Today, although House members average more than fifty years of age, a very young candidate can sometimes get elected. In 2000, voters in Florida's Twelfth District sent Adam Putnam, a twenty-six-year-old Republican, to the House of Representatives.

▼ **Members are sworn in when a new Congress begins, in January of each odd-numbered year.**

As laid out in Article I, Section 3, the requirements for election to the Senate are somewhat stricter. Each senator must be at least thirty years old and must have been a U.S. citizen for at least nine years. Like House members, senators must have been living in the state in which they were elected. Senators tend to be older, on average, than members of the House. One reason for this is that many politicians serve several terms in the House before they seek a seat in the Senate.

Members of the House must run for reelection every two years. The framers believed this would allow the House to respond quickly to changes in the mood of the people. The Senate, on the other hand, is shielded from rapid changes in public opinion. Each senator serves a six-year term, and only one-third of Senate terms expire in any given two-year period.

The framers went even further in trying to protect the Senate from sudden shifts in the public mood. As originally written, Article I, Section 3 of the Constitution provided that members of the Senate be chosen by the state legislatures. This system was changed by the Seventeenth **Amendment**, which was passed by Congress in 1912 and **ratified** by the states in 1913. Today, senators—like members of the House—are directly elected by the people of their home states.

The Term Limits Movement

The Constitution sets no limit on the number of terms a representative or senator may serve. In the early 1990s, a growing number of voters thought this was not a good idea.

Voters in about two dozen states passed laws limiting the number of terms their U.S. senators and representatives could serve. In 1995, however, the Supreme Court ruled on the issue. By a majority of five votes to four, the Court struck down these state laws. The only way to limit congressional terms, the Court ruled, was to change the U.S. Constitution.

⬟ Protesters like the one shown in this photo have succeeded in imposing term limits on state and local officials, but not on members of Congress.

Article I, Section 6 provides for members of Congress to be paid for their work. When the House and Senate first met in 1789, each member of Congress received six dollars per day. Salaries have gone up since then, and each pay raise has brought a new round of grumbling from taxpayers. As of 2002, the base pay for each House and Senate member was $150,000 a year plus expenses.

POWERS OF CONGRESS

The Constitution outlines the powers of Congress in Article I, Section 8. Many of the provisions in this section deal with the "power of the purse"—the ability of Congress to raise and spend money. The Constitution allows Congress to:

▼ **The Constitution gives Congress the power to print money (below) and regulate shipping (bottom).**

- Collect taxes of various kinds
- Print money
- Borrow money
- Raise and maintain an army and navy
- Pay debts and provide for the "common defense and general welfare of the United States"
- Regulate trade with foreign countries and between the states.

None of these powers is unlimited. Because the framers wanted to make sure that no branch of the U.S. government became too powerful, they set up a system of checks and balances. This system was designed to prevent Congress from gaining too much power over the president and the courts, and the courts or the president from gaining too much power over Congress. The Constitution also limits both the power Congress has over the states and the power the states have over Congress.

Although most powers of Congress are given jointly to both the House and the Senate, the Constitution does spell out some differences between the two bodies. For example, all **bills** (see Chapter 5) involving taxes must start out in the House. The Senate, and only the Senate, has the job of approving or rejecting the president's choices for the Supreme Court and other high offices. Similarly, approval of a treaty requires a two-thirds vote of the Senate; no House vote is needed.

One of the most difficult problems facing the framers was whether it should be Congress or the president that has the power to make war. The Constitution deals with this problem by making the president commander in chief of the armed forces, but giving Congress the power to declare war. The last time Congress issued a formal declaration of war was during World War II, after Japan attacked the United States Navy base at Pearl Harbor, Hawaii, on December 7, 1941. Since then, U.S. troops have fought and died in Korea, Vietnam, Somalia, Afghanistan, and many other places (see Chapter 6), despite the lack of declarations of war by Congress.

Jeannette Rankin

The first woman to serve in Congress was Jeannette Rankin. Running as a Republican, she was elected to the U.S. House of Representatives by Montana voters in 1916. She won her race at a time when women did not even have the right to vote.

Rankin is famous for another reason. She was not only a supporter of women's rights but also a lifelong peace activist. In 1917, when Congress debated whether the United States should enter World War I, Rankin was one of only fifty to vote no, saying "I want to stand by my country, but I cannot vote for war."

▲ **Jeannette Rankin**

Rankin left the House in 1919, after serving only one term. Twenty-one years later, she again ran for the House from Montana, and again she was elected. In 1941, she was the only member of Congress to vote against U.S. entry into World War II. "As a woman I can't go to war," she said, "and I refuse to send anyone else." Some people were so angry about her vote that, after casting it, she had to lock herself in a telephone booth and call for security guards to keep the mob away.

Chapter Three

GETTING ELECTED AND REELECTED

▼ **Representative J. C. Watts (second from right) was the lone black Republican member of the 107th Congress. With him at this 1997 news conference were three other Republicans (from left to right): Senator Ben Nighthorse Campbell, a Native American; Speaker of the House Newt Gingrich; and Republican National Committee Co-Chair Pat Harrison.**

When Jeannette Rankin entered the House of Representatives for her first term in 1917, she was the only woman among 434 men. When she returned to the House for a second term in 1941, the chamber had seven other female members, and there was one woman serving in the Senate. Sixty years later, the 107th Congress had sixty-one women in the House and thirteen women in the Senate.

Congress has changed in other ways as well. The first black member of Congress, Hiram Revels of Mississippi, was elected to the Senate as a Republican in 1870. The 107th Congress had thirty-six members who were black. All of them were in the House, and all but one of them were Democrats. The same Congress also included among its members nineteen Latinos; seven Asians, Native Hawaiians, or other Pacific Islanders; and two Native Americans.

INCUMBENTS RULE

What has not changed is the fact that the great majority of House and Senate members are middle-aged white males, just as they were in earlier centuries. One reason why change has come so slowly is the power of incumbents—members of Congress who already hold their seats.

It is much harder to be elected to Congress for the first time than it is to be reelected. This is especially true in the House, where in most election years at least 90 percent of incumbents who run for another term win their races. Many incumbents have the advantage of running from "safe" states or districts —areas that lean either

strongly Republican or strongly Democratic. If these members remain on good terms with their own parties, they can hold their seats for a very long time.

Incumbents have other advantages that help them hold onto their jobs. In addition to their salaries, they receive money that covers the costs of having a staff, traveling to and from home, and opening offices in their home districts. They can send out mailings without having to pay postage. Another benefit of incumbency is that under the **seniority system**, longtime incumbents usually get to chair the most important committees. They can use

▲ **Dianne Feinstein of California, a Democrat, is one of more than a dozen women who have served in the Senate in recent years. She helped pass a ban on weapons like the AR-15 assault rifle she holds in this photo.**

◄ **Some of the most senior members of Congress were chosen to investigate whether the terrorist attacks of September 11, 2001, could have been prevented. At the microphone is Senator Bob Graham of Florida.**

their seniority to work on issues of particular importance to voters in their home states or districts.

Incumbents also find it much easier than challengers to raise campaign money. In 1999–2000, for example, the average incumbent in a House race raised nearly six dollars for every one dollar raised by a challenger.

OPEN SEATS

An **open seat** is a seat in the House of Representatives or the Senate for which there is no incumbent. Open seats typically occur when a member of Congress dies or decides to retire. These vacancies can also result when an incumbent loses a **party primary** or when a member of the House gives up a seat to run for the Senate. In an election for an open seat, no candidate has the advantage of being an incumbent. For this reason, open seats offer the minority party in the House or Senate the best chance of picking up enough seats to become the majority party.

The competition to win control of open seats produces some of the fiercest and most expensive battles in any election year. In 2000, for example, the Democratic and Republican candidates for U.S. senator from New York spent a combined total of more than $70 million in the race that was won by Hillary Rodham Clinton, the wife of President Bill Clinton. Knowing that control of Congress may be at stake, party loyalists from all over the country may donate money to give their party's candidate the edge.

They Also Serve

Joining the 435 regular members of the House are five special members—one each from Puerto Rico, the U.S. Virgin Islands, Guam, American Samoa, and Washington, D.C. These five members, called delegates, can vote in House committees. (See Chapter 5.) They can also make speeches from the House floor. But they cannot vote when the whole House meets to approve or reject bills or amendments.

CONGRESS AND THE CENSUS

Every ten years the United States counts how many people are living in each state. The most recent population count, or census, was conducted in 2000; the next one will be held in 2010. The census does not affect the Senate because the number of senators does not depend on the population of each state. But it has an unsettling effect on the House.

Early in United States history, as the nation's population increased, the House simply added new seats to represent the growing number of citizens. Between 1789 and 1900, the House grew in size from 65 to 391. Early in the twentieth century, Congress put a limit on the number of representatives in the House, to keep it from getting too big. This would have posed no problem if all states and districts increased in population at the same rate. But, in fact, some states grew much faster than others. For example, Florida, one of the fastest-growing states, has more than tripled its number of seats in the House since 1950. Because the total

⬆ **In 2000, Rick Lazio, a Republican, and Hillary Rodham Clinton, a Democrat, spent more than $70 million while competing for an open U.S. Senate seat.**

🌱 **Census takers try to count everyone, including these homeless people on the streets of Philadelphia. Results of the census reshape the House of Representatives every ten years.**

number of seats has been fixed at 435, while Florida gained seats, some slower-growing states had to lose seats. This process is known as **reapportionment**.

As a state gains or loses seats in the House, it also gains or loses congressional districts. In either case, the map of the state's districts needs to be redrawn. When a state adds seats, new districts are carved out of existing districts. When a state loses seats, existing districts may need to be combined. This process is called **redistricting**.

Reapportionment and redistricting can make life unpleasant for House members. When districts are redrawn, a member who was in a "safe" district two years ago may now face a much stronger challenge. When a state loses seats, an incumbent who wants to stay in the House may have no choice but to run against another incumbent.

Members of the U.S. House of Representatives

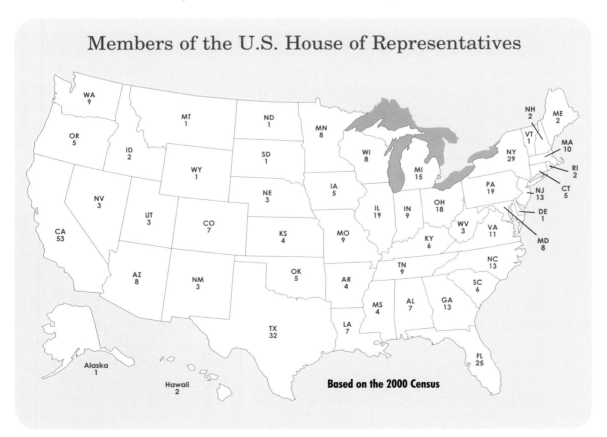

Based on the 2000 Census

HOUSE AND SENATE

For most things that Congress does, action by both the House and the Senate is required. No bill may be passed without the approval of both chambers. Each year, the House and Senate meet jointly to hear the president deliver the **State of the Union** address. Joint meetings are also held at other times, such as when the president or—less often—a foreign leader asks to address Congress.

In some cases, however, the Constitution gives very different roles to the House and Senate. A clear example of this occurs in the process of impeachment—the procedure by which a president can be charged with a crime or abuse of power and removed from office if found guilty. Impeachment begins in the House, which brings charges against the president. Each of the charges, which are called articles of impeachment, needs a majority vote to pass the House. The Senate's job is to put the president on trial for these charges. The president cannot be removed unless the Senate finds him guilty of at least one charge by a two-thirds majority.

⬡ **In 1998, the House Judiciary Committee voted to recommend that the whole House impeach President Clinton.**

Different by Design

James Madison started out as a House member before becoming the nation's fourth president. He explained that the framers intended the Senate and House to serve as checks and balances on each other as well as on the other branches of government:

In republican government, the legislative authority necessarily predominates. The remedy for this inconveniency is, to divide the legislature into different branches; and to render them, by different modes of election, and different principles of action, as little connected with each other, as the nature of their common functions and their common dependence on the society, will admit.

⬡ **James Madison**

▲ **Vice President Dick Cheney (center) and House Speaker J. Dennis Hastert (right) applaud President George W. Bush's 2002 State of the Union address.**

▼ **Members of Congress attend a joint session in the House chamber. Invited guests fill the visitors gallery.**

CHANGING TRADITIONS

As originally written, the Constitution made the House much closer to the people than the Senate. (See Chapter 2.) The Constitution also gave the House a leading role in raising and spending money. For these reasons, the framers thought the House was the more important of the two chambers. They believed that the best minds and most skillful debaters would want to serve in the House rather than the Senate.

They were soon proved wrong. By the 1830s, a French visitor, Alexis de Tocqueville, described the differences between the Senate and House this way:

> *On entering the House of Representatives in Washington one is struck by the vulgar demeanor of that great assembly. . . . At a few yards' distance from this spot is the door of the Senate, which contains within a small space a large proportion of the most celebrated men of America.*

One reason for this development was the difference in the size of the two bodies. Although the Senate added two members each time a new state joined the Union, the House grew at a much more rapid rate. When Tocqueville visited the United States, the House was more than four times larger than the Senate. The same holds true today.

Because of the greater size of the House, discipline is much more important. Strict rules govern which bills can be brought up for debate and how much they can be changed. Most members cannot talk very long or show much independence. In the smaller Senate, on the other hand, individual members have much greater power. They can talk at much greater length—and they usually do.

HOW THE HOUSE IS ORGANIZED

The most powerful figure in the House of Representatives is the **speaker of the House**. The House elects its speaker by majority vote, and the speaker, therefore, is always a member of the majority party. Assisting the speaker are the majority leader, who is second in command, and the majority **whip**, whose job it is to try to make sure that party members vote the same way on important issues.

Mr. Speaker

The speaker of the House is usually one of the best known members of Congress. Powerful House speakers have included Sam Rayburn of Texas, in the 1940s and 1950s, and Thomas P. "Tip" O'Neill of Massachusetts, in the 1980s; both were Democrats.

The most important speaker of the House in recent years was Newt Gingrich, the Georgia Republican who came up with the plan that led his party to victory in the election of November 1994. That win gave Republicans their first House majority in four decades.

▲ J. Dennis Hastert, a Republican from Illinois, became speaker of the House in 1999.

The proper way to address the speaker of the House is "Mr. Speaker." No woman has ever been speaker of the House. The highest-ranking woman in the history of Congress is Nancy Pelosi of California. In November 2002, Democrats in the House chose her for the top-ranking party position, minority leader.

The minority party in the House chooses the minority leader and the minority whip.

Being a minority member in the House is often very frustrating. The majority party gets to decide which bills come to a vote and when each vote will be held. The majority also controls every House committee and sub-committee. The life of a minority member is especially tough when the majority party holds onto power for a very long time, as the Democrats did from 1955 through 1994.

HOW THE SENATE IS ORGANIZED

The Constitution gives to the vice president of the United States the job of presiding over the Senate. In practice, the vice president appears in the Senate very rarely and casts a vote only to break a tie. When the vice president is absent, the Constitution assigns the task of presiding over the Senate to the **president pro tempore**. This title is based on the Latin term *pro tempore*, which sounds like "temporary" and means "for the time being." The president pro tempore is usually the longest-serving member of the majority party. The title carries much honor but very little power.

The most powerful member of the Senate is the majority leader, who is chosen by the majority party. As in the House, the minority party chooses a minority leader, and each party has a whip. Because Senate rules protect the minority party much more than do those of the House, little can be done in the Senate unless the leaders of the two parties work together.

Normally, the party that starts out with a majority when the first session begins keeps control of the Senate for a full two years. The 2000 election was so close, however, that when the Senate met in January it was split fifty-fifty between Republicans and Democrats. Under the Constitution, Vice President Dick Cheney, a Republican, was required to break the tie. Since Cheney

▲ Nancy Pelosi, the highest-ranking woman in the history of Congress, shows off the real whip she got as a gift when she was elected to the post of minority whip in 2001 by House Democrats. The Democrats chose her as their minority leader after the November 2002 election.

voted with his own party, Senator Trent Lott, a Republican from Mississippi, became majority leader, and Senator Tom Daschle, a Democrat from South Dakota, became minority leader.

Only a few months later, Senator Jim Jeffords of Vermont shocked his fellow Republicans by deciding to leave the party and become an independent. That left the Senate with fifty Democrats but only forty-nine Republicans. With the Democrats now in the majority (and Jeffords siding with them), Daschle became majority leader and Lott became minority leader.

Republicans made gains in the election of November 2002. As a result, when the 108th Congress met in January 2003, Republicans controlled both the Senate and the House.

⏶ **Senate Democrats, including Edward Kennedy (right), cheered Jim Jeffords (left) when he decided to leave the Republican Party.**

Other Parts of Congress

The following agencies also belong to the legislative branch.

- **Library of Congress:** Founded in 1800, the Library of Congress is the largest library in the world, with more than 18 million books and over 100 million other items.

- **Government Printing Office:** The GPO was established in 1860. It publishes the *Congressional Record* (the official account of debates and votes in the House and Senate) and has published millions of other documents.

- **General Accounting Office:** Set up in 1921, the GAO guards against waste and fraud in spending by the executive branch.

- **Congressional Budget Office:** Since 1974, the CBO has provided Congress with information about the money raised and spent by the federal government.

⏶ **The Great Hall of the Library of Congress**

Chapter Five

HOW A BILL BECOMES A LAW

Over the two-year lifespan of each Congress, thousands of bills may be proposed. A few hundred of these pass both the House and the Senate and are signed into law by the president. The other bills die when a congressional term ends.

Any member of Congress can introduce a bill for debate. But only a member with skill and influence can guide a bill from the early stage in which it is discussed and debated through the vote that can make it a law.

EARLY STAGES

▼ First elected to the Senate in 1962, Edward Kennedy of Massachusetts has used his seniority and national influence to help pass many bills and block others.

The life of a bill begins when it is introduced by a member of Congress. The member who introduces the bill is known as its sponsor. Each bill is numbered in the order in which it is introduced. For example, a bill with the number H.R. 10 would be the tenth bill introduced in the House during the current Congress; a measure called S. 25 would be the twenty-fifth bill introduced in the Senate.

Members of Congress usually do not write the bills they introduce. Many bills are actually written by the executive branch or by business and labor groups. During the 2000 presidential campaign, for example, George W. Bush pledged to cut taxes for many Americans. After the new Congress met in 2001, the president's staff drew up a specific plan to reduce taxes, which was introduced as a series of bills in the House.

What Is Pork Barrel Spending?

Incumbents who run for reelection like to boast about how much they have done for their districts. Highways, dams, schools, sewage treatment plants, jet fighters, and aircraft carriers—federal dollars pay for all of these. Voters usually reelect members of Congress who make sure that lots of federal dollars are spent in their home districts.

At the same time, voters and members of Congress often complain about wasteful government projects. Such projects are often called "pork," and the money that funds them is labeled "pork barrel spending."

Some members of Congress have tried hard to cut down on pork barrel spending. More often, however, members agree to vote for each other's favorite local programs, as a way of winning support for their own.

▲ **Wisconsin Senator William Proxmire gave "Golden Fleece Awards" to projects he accused of wasting taxpayers' money.**

COMMITTEE ACTION

Almost every bill introduced in Congress is sent to a committee for detailed discussion. Each chamber of Congress has about twenty committees, and each committee may have several subcommittees. One of the most important committees in the House is Ways and Means, which was the first to consider the bills that made up the Bush tax plan.

▼ **House and Senate committees usually hold hearings before voting on a bill.**

A committee or subcommittee will usually hold hearings on a bill. During hearings, witnesses read or submit statements they have written in advance about the strengths and weaknesses of the bill. They also answer questions from committee members. Witnesses at these hearings

HOW A BILL BECOMES LAW

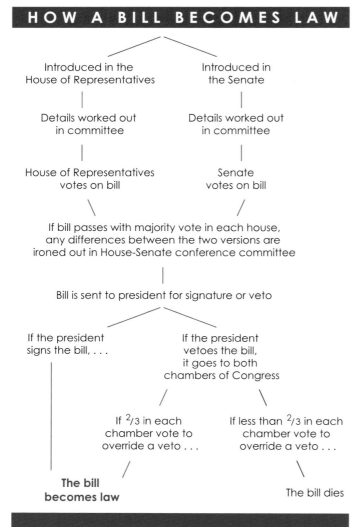

Introduced in the House of Representatives — Introduced in the Senate

Details worked out in committee — Details worked out in committee

House of Representatives votes on bill — Senate votes on bill

If bill passes with majority vote in each house, any differences between the two versions are ironed out in House-Senate conference committee

Bill is sent to president for signature or veto

If the president signs the bill, . . . — If the president vetoes the bill, it goes to both chambers of Congress

If $2/3$ in each chamber vote to override a veto . . . — If less than $2/3$ in each chamber vote to override a veto . . .

The bill becomes law — The bill dies

▲ **The House has an electronic voting system that displays the results as the votes are cast.**

often include heads of interest groups and government agencies that will be affected by the bill.

After hearings have been held, the committee members discuss the bill and make changes. This is called marking up the bill. If the revised bill wins a majority vote in the committee, it stands a good chance of passing the whole House or Senate. If it fails to win a majority in the committee, the bill usually dies right there.

FLOOR ACTION

After a bill is approved by one of the House committees, it is submitted to the Rules Committee. This powerful committee decides when the bill will reach the House floor, how long it will be debated, and how many amendments may be offered. In the Senate, the majority and minority leaders usually decide the order in which particular bills will be brought up.

One important difference between the House and the Senate is that the Senate does not like to limit debate. Senators often debate measures for days on end. During the course of a debate, dozens of amendments may be offered.

Some amendments are designed to improve the bill. thers are offered by opponents of the bill, in order to weaken it or reduce its chances of passage.

The rules of the Senate allow the opponents of a bill to delay a vote for a very long time, but not forever. If supporters of a bill feel they have enough votes to cut off debate, they can move for what is called a vote on cloture. A majority of fifty-one votes is enough to pass any ordinary bill, but a vote on cloture requires a sixty-vote majority. Once a cloture vote passes, approval of the bill is almost certain. If the cloture vote fails—and more than half do— the bill usually dies, and the Senate moves on to other business.

FINAL STAGES

If exactly the same bill wins majorities in both the House and the Senate, it goes directly to the president for signing. But if the original bill has been changed by either the House or the Senate or both, the two versions must go to a conference committee. The conference committee includes majority and minority members from both chambers of Congress.

In theory, the conference committee is only supposed to iron out the differences between the two different versions of the bill. In practice, if the differences

What Is a Filibuster?

A **filibuster** is a series of very long speeches designed to prevent a bill from coming to a vote. Strom Thurmond, a Republican from South Carolina, gave the longest speech in Senate history—a total of twenty-four hours and eighteen minutes—as part of a 1957 filibuster.

⚊ This photo shows Senator Strom Thurmond (gesturing at left) in 1957, just after he set the all-time Senate filibuster record. He was trying to block passage of a civil rights bill.

between the House and Senate versions are very great, the conference committee may rewrite much of the bill. The White House and various interest groups also weigh in, hoping once again to influence the bill before it comes up for a final vote.

After the House and Senate have each approved the final compromise version of the bill, it is sent to the president. If the president signs it within ten days (excluding Sundays) after he receives it, the bill becomes law.

If the president does not wish to sign the bill, he has several other options. He can reject, or **veto**, the bill, telling Congress his reasons for opposing it. Or, he can do nothing. After the required ten-day period, if Congress is still in session, the bill automatically becomes law, even without the president's signature. If Congress is no longer in session at the end of ten days, the bill dies. This last case is called a pocket veto.

A bill vetoed by the president can still become law if both houses vote to override the veto. A vote to override requires a two-thirds majority in each chamber of Congress. If either chamber falls short of a two-thirds majority, the veto is sustained, and the bill does not become law. In practice, few vetoes are overridden.

What Is a Lame Duck Session?

In even-numbered years, Congress tries to complete its work several weeks before Election Day, in early November. This is so the members can head home to campaign. Sometimes, however, so much work remains unfinished that the members have to return to Washington for a special session later in November. This is called a "lame duck" session because some members who take part in it have already lost on Election Day and will be replaced when a new Congress meets the following January.

Congress met for a lame duck session after the election of November 2002, while Democrats still controlled the Senate. Some bills were passed during this session, but many important matters were postponed. This is because Republicans did not want to discuss them until the new Congress, when they would hold majorities in both the Senate and the House.

LANDMARK LEGISLATION

Congressional actions affect every area of American life. Laws passed by Congress have an impact on which wildlife areas will be preserved, which foods are approved as safe to eat, and how many students can afford to go to college. Whether Americans can buy a home, pay for health care, or pay their bills when they retire—these matters, too, are affected by what Congress does.

Among the hundreds of bills passed by Congress each year, a few stand out as landmarks. These important laws make the United States stronger by helping the nation meet new challenges both at home and overseas.

EQUAL RIGHTS

During the 1950s and 1960s, many Americans came to realize that their country did not treat everybody fairly. Whites got better treatment than blacks. Men were treated better than women. And men and women with disabilities did not have the same rights as people without disabilities. Congress took steps to deal with each of these problems.

One of the most far-reaching measures ever passed by Congress was the Civil Rights Act of 1964. This law required hotels, motels, restaurants, movie theaters, sports arenas, and other public places to treat all customers in exactly the same way, regardless of race, skin color, religion, or ethnic group. In order

▼ Civil rights leaders marched in Washington in the early 1960s to pressure Congress to help black Americans gain equality with whites.

to pass this law, Republican and Democratic leaders worked together to break a filibuster by senators opposed to civil rights legislation that had tied up the Senate for months.

Although the Civil Rights Act of 1964 was intended mainly to help black people win equality with whites, it also helped to expand the rights of women. Another major step toward women's equality came eight years later, when Congress passed Title IX of the Education Amendments Act of 1972. (The "IX" is the Roman numeral for "nine.") Title IX required all schools receiving federal funds to treat females and males equally. Because of Title IX, millions of girls and women are now able to play on public school sports teams.

▼ In a ceremony at the White House in 1990, President George H. W. Bush signed a law to help Americans with disabilities.

Congress took a third major step in providing equal rights for all Americans when it passed the Americans with Disabilities Act in 1990. This landmark law, also known as ADA, protects people who have difficulty seeing, hearing, speaking, walking, learning, or performing other important daily activities. ADA requires companies and state and local government agencies to break down many of the barriers that prevent people with disabilities from receiving fair treatment.

Bob Dole

One of the main supporters of the Americans with Disabilities Act was Senator Bob Dole, a Kansas Republican. He knew the kinds of problems people with disabilities face every day. In 1945, during World War II, Dole was badly injured while fighting in northern Italy. The future senator permanently lost the use of his right arm, and his left hand was also damaged. Dole was elected to the Senate in 1968 and was minority leader when the ADA passed in 1990.

MAKING DEMOCRACY WORK

Until the mid-1960s, the whites who controlled politics in the South enforced local laws that made it difficult for blacks to vote. These white leaders feared they would lose their political power if black people voted in large numbers.

In 1965, Congress passed the Voting Rights Act, which ended many of the unfair tactics that had been used to keep blacks from voting. The new law was a tremendous success. Many more black people voted and were elected to public office. Barriers to voting have also been removed for Latinos, Asians, and Native Americans.

Complicated voting rules can often discourage new voters. In 1993, Congress tried to remedy this problem by passing the National Voter Registration Act. This law, also known as Motor Voter, makes it as easy to sign up, or register, to vote as it is to apply for a driver's license. Motor Voter also allows voters to register by mail and at many government offices.

Something else that discourages people from voting is the belief that big money has corrupted politics in the United States. Americans who think the system is corrupt point to the gigantic sums of money that candidates and political parties need to raise and spend in order to win elections. After years of debate, Congress took an important first step to deal with this problem by passing the McCain-Feingold Bill in 2002. This law—which is

▲ Title IX is the law that makes sure girls have the same opportunities as boys to play school sports.

▼ Senator John McCain (left), a Republican, and Senator Russell Feingold (right foreground), a Democrat, worked together to help reduce the power of big money in U.S. politics.

named for Senator John McCain, an Arizona Republican, and Senator Russell Feingold, a Wisconsin Democrat—does not curb spending by candidates, but it sharply limits the sources and amounts of money given to political parties.

▼ National Guard soldiers were placed at airports after September 11, 2001.

DEFENDING THE NATION

Whenever U.S. troops are facing danger overseas, most U.S. citizens want to rally round the commander in chief—the president of the United States. Most members of Congress also want to support the president. They understand, however, that the framers had a reason for giving Congress—and not the president—the power to declare war. (See Chapter 2.) The framers wanted to make sure that no president would send troops into war without seeking approval from Congress and the people.

From the mid-1960s through the mid-1970s, tens of thousands of U.S. soldiers fought and died in Asia during the Vietnam War. Many Americans supported the war, but as the years went by, an increasing number did not. Members of the Senate and House believed that a series of presidents had gotten the United States deeper and deeper into war without properly asking permission from Congress.

▲ Deep divisions about the Vietnam War and how the United States got into it led Congress to pass the War Powers Act in 1973.

To prevent this from happening again, Congress, in 1973, passed the War Powers Act. President Richard M. Nixon vetoed the bill, but Congress overrode his veto. The War Powers Act requires a president to let Congress know within forty-eight hours when U.S. troops are sent into combat. It also puts a time limit on how long a president can keep troops in combat before asking Congress to approve the action. Although presidents have complained about the law, they have been careful to consult with Congress anyway.

Congress moved quickly to defend the nation after September 11, 2001, when terrorists destroyed the World Trade Center in New York City and damaged the Pentagon near Washington, D.C. Fulfilling its obligations under the War Powers Act, Congress approved this statement on September 14:

> *The president is author-ized to use all necessary and appropriate force against those nations, organizations, or persons he determines planned, authorized, committed, or aided the terrorist attacks that occurred on September 11, 2001, or harbored such organizations or persons, in order to prevent any future acts of international terrorism against the United States by such nations, organizations, or persons.*

Since September 2001, Congress has been called on to take many other actions. Some of these, such as the USA Patriot Act, have given the executive branch new powers to spy on, arrest, and hold people suspected of being terrorists. Courts are reviewing the new laws to see whether Congress did the right thing or gave the president too much power.

🔺 **While firefighters and others worked to save lives and clear the ruins of the World Trade Center, Congress and the president took immediate action to defend the nation.**

Chapter Seven

CONGRESS IN THE SPOTLIGHT

The main job of Congress is to make laws. But Congress also makes news in other ways. The Senate has a special role in deciding whether to approve or reject the president's choices for the Supreme Court and other high government jobs. Congressional committees have helped to uncover wrongdoing by the executive branch. At times, the House and Senate must investigate and punish members of Congress who have acted improperly.

INVESTIGATIONS

Congress investigates all kinds of questions, from the most important matters of foreign policy to whether raunchy rock and rap records should carry warning labels. One of the most important probes conducted by Congress was an investigation of the Watergate scandal. The scandal began on June 17, 1972, when five burglars were arrested while trying to break into Democratic National Committee headquarters in the Watergate building, located in Washington, D.C.

▲ When Tipper Gore appeared before a congressional committee in 1985, she called for warning labels on certain kinds of pop music.

The president at that time was Richard Nixon, a Republican. Congress wanted to find out how much Nixon knew about the burglary and about the people who carried it out. A special Senate committee was set up in 1973 to find out whether the president had abused his power. The committee found evidence of illegal and improper acts by Nixon and his staff. The following year, the House Judiciary Committee held hearings to decide whether Nixon should be impeached. As the evidence against him mounted, Nixon resigned from the presidency on August 9, 1974.

Help or Harm?

Senator Sam Ervin, a Democrat from North Carolina, headed the Senate Watergate Committee. He warned that the power to investigate wrongdoing was a dangerous weapon that could be used for good or evil:

> *The congressional investigation can be an instrument of freedom. Or it can be freedom's **scourge**. A legislative inquiry can serve as the tool to pry open the barriers that hide governmental corruption. … Or it can debase our principles, invade the privacy of our citizens, and afford a platform for **demagogues** and the rankest partisans.*

▲ Senator Sam Ervin (right) chaired the Senate Watergate Committee.

IMPEACHMENT TRIALS

Two presidents have been impeached by the House: Andrew Johnson in 1868 and Bill Clinton in 1998. Johnson became president after the **Civil War**. The specific charge against him was that he had improperly fired a cabinet officer. But the real reason for his impeachment was that Johnson, a southerner, wanted to be more lenient with the South than Congress did. Johnson escaped conviction in his Senate trial by a single vote.

One hundred and thirty years later, the House of Representatives impeached Bill Clinton for trying to cover up an affair

▼ Andrew Johnson was the first president to be impeached.

▲ **This 1868 sketch shows Andrew Johnson's impeachment trial in the Senate. A single vote saved the president from being forced out of office.**

with Monica Lewinsky, a young woman who worked in the White House. The House of Representatives charged Clinton with lying under oath and involving others in a cover-up. As in the Johnson case, the Senate refused to convict the president.

Congress has the power to impeach and remove from office not just the president but also other high officials. In addition to Johnson and Clinton, twelve judges, one cabinet officer, and one U.S. senator have been charged by the House and tried in the Senate. Seven of the judges were convicted and removed from office.

CONFIRMATION HEARINGS

Each president chooses many hundreds of people for high office, including Supreme Court justices and the heads of cabinet departments. The president submits all of these names to the Senate. In most cases, a Senate committee promptly holds a hearing, which is usually friendly and brief, and the official is quickly confirmed. Nominees almost always have smooth sailing when the same party controls both the presidency and the Senate.

Once in a while, however, a nominee faces serious opposition. Sometimes opponents will raise questions about a candidate's fitness for office. For example, when President George H. W. Bush tried to appoint John Tower as secretary of defense in 1989, opponents charged that Tower drank too much and had other personal problems. Tower, a Republican and a former U.S. senator from Texas, was only the ninth cabinet nominee in U.S. history to be defeated in the Senate. Of the fifty-three senators who voted against him, fifty-two were Democrats.

Robert Bork, who was chosen for the Supreme Court by President Ronald Reagan in 1987, was another nominee who lost in the Senate. Bork, a well-known judge and legal thinker, held very conservative views on issues such as women's rights. Fifty-eight senators (including six Republicans) voted against him, and only forty-two voted in favor.

Another Supreme Court nominee, Clarence Thomas, was confirmed by the Senate only after a ferocious fight. Thomas, a federal judge with a conservative record, was named to the Court by President George H. W. Bush in 1991. During Thomas's confirmation hearings, Anita Hill, a lawyer who worked with him the early 1980s, said he had sexually harassed her. Thomas angrily denied the charge and called the hearings a "high-tech lynching." The dispute between Thomas and Hill, both of whom were African-American, was front-page news all around the world.

⚊ **John Ashcroft, a former senator, faced tough questions from some members of the Senate Judiciary Committee in early 2001, but the Senate confirmed him as attorney general.**

▲ Public support dwindled for Senator Joseph McCarthy (standing at center) after Senate hearings in 1954.

CLEANING HOUSE

Article I, Section 5 of the Constitution makes each chamber of Congress the judge of its own members. When a House member does wrong, it is up to the House to decide what action to take. Similarly, when a senator misbehaves, the Senate has the responsibility of deciding which punishment to impose.

A decision by the Senate in 1954 to condemn Senator Joseph McCarthy hastened the end of a frightening era in American politics. McCarthy, a Wisconsin Republican, was first elected to the Senate in 1946. This was a time when tensions were rising between the United States and the Soviet Union, a communist country. Based on flimsy

C-SPAN

The Cable-Satellite Public Affairs Network, or C-SPAN, is a private organization funded by the cable TV industry. It began offering live daily coverage of the House of Representatives in 1979; live daily coverage of the Senate began in 1986. Today, C-SPAN provides round-the-clock public affairs programs on TV, radio, and the World Wide Web.

evidence, McCarthy charged hundreds of U.S. government officials with being disloyal to their country. When he accused the U.S. Army of "coddling communists," his fellow senators had heard enough. Televised hearings exposed McCarthy's recklessness, and his public support dwindled. He died in 1957, a lonely and bitter man.

The House went through a period of scandal and turmoil in late 1980s and the 1990s. In 1989, Jim Wright, a Texas Democrat, became the first speaker of the House to be forced to resign in disgrace during the middle of his term. Wright was accused of violating House rules on accepting money and gifts from outside sources. One of Wright's main accusers was Newt Gingrich, who became Republican whip in 1989. Democrats had their chance for revenge in 1997 after Gingrich, who had become speaker of the House, was charged with violating ethics rules. The House voted to fine Gingrich $300,000, but he was allowed to keep his position as House speaker.

▼ **Representative Newt Gingrich, who helped Republicans win control of the House in 1994, was later punished for violating ethics rules.**

The harshest punishment the House or Senate can impose on a member is expulsion. Except during the Civil War, when fourteen senators and three representatives were expelled, this penalty has rarely been used. No senator has been forced out since 1862; two members, however, resigned when threatened with expulsion. In the House, two members, both Democrats, have been expelled since the end of the Civil War: Michael "Ozzie" Myers of Pennsylvania in 1980 and James Traficant of Ohio in 2002. Before the House voted to expel them, each congressman was convicted in federal court on bribery charges.

POLITICAL PARTIES IN CONGRESS, 1901-2003

Congress	Years	SENATE Total	D	R	Other	HOUSE OF REPRESENTATIVES Total	D	R	Other
57th	1901-03	90	29	56	5	357	153	198	6
58th	1903-05	90	32	58		386	178	207	1
59th	1905-07	90	32	58		386	136	250	
60th	1907-09	92	29	61	2	386	164	222	
61st	1909-11	92	32	59	1	391	172	219	
62nd	1911-13	92	42	49	1	391	228	162	1
63rd	1913-15	96	51	44	1	435	290	127	18
64th	1915-17	96	56	39	1	435	231	193	11
65th	1917-19	96	53	42	1	435	210[1]	216	9
66th	1919-21	96	47	48	1	435	191	237	7
67th	1921-23	96	37	59		435	132	300	3
68th	1923-25	96	43	51	2	435	207	225	3
69th	1925-27	96	40	54	2	435	183	247	5
70th	1927-29	96	47	48	1	435	195	237	3
71st	1929-31	96	39	56	1	435	163	267	5
72nd	1931-33	96	47	48	1	435	216[2]	218	1
73rd	1933-35	96	59	36	1	435	313	117	5
74th	1935-37	96	69	25	2	435	322	103	10
75th	1937-39	96	75	17	4	435	333	89	13
76th	1939-41	96	69	23	4	435	262	169	4
77th	1941-43	96	66	28	2	435	267	162	6
78th	1943-45	96	57	38	1	435	222	209	4
79th	1945-47	96	57	38	1	435	243	190	2
80th	1947-49	96	45	51		435	188	246	1
81st	1949-51	96	54	42		435	263	171	1
82nd	1951-53	96	48	47	1	435	234	199	2

Congress	Years	SENATE				HOUSE OF REPRESENTATIVES			
		Total	D	R	Other	Total	D	R	Other
83rd	1953-55	96	46	48	2	435	213	221	1
84th	1955-57	96	48	47	1	435	232	203	
85th	1957-59	96	49	47		435	234	201	
86th	1959-61	98	64	34		436	283	153	
87th	1961-63	100	64	36		437	262	175	
88th	1963-65	100	67	33		435	258	176	1
89th	1965-67	100	68	32		435	295	140	
90th	1967-69	100	64	36		435	248	187	
91st	1969-71	100	58	42		435	243	192	
92nd	1971-73	100	54	44	2	435	255	180	
93rd	1973-75	100	56	42	2	435	242	192	1
94th	1975-77	100	60	37	2	435	291	144	1
95th	1977-79	100	61	38	1	435	292	143	
96th	1979-81	100	58	41	1	435	277	158	
97th	1981-83	100	46	53	1	435	242	192	1
98th	1983-85	100	46	54		435	269	166	
99th	1985-87	100	47	53		435	253	182	
100th	1987-89	100	55	45		435	258	177	
101st	1989-91	100	55	45		435	260	175	
102nd	1991-93	100	56	44		435	267	167	1
103rd	1993-95	100	57	43		435	258	176	1
104th	1995-97	100	48	52		435	204	230	1
105th	1997-99	100	45	55		435	207	227	1
106th	1999-2001	100	45	55		435	211	223	1
107th	2001-03	100	50	50[3]		435	212	221	2
108th[4]	2003-05	100	48	51	1	435	205	229	1

NOTES: In years shaded with red, Republicans controlled the presidency and both houses of Congress. In years shaded with blue, Democrats controlled the presidency and both houses of Congress. All figures reflect party totals immediately after the election. Figures for "other" include vacant seats and independents. (1) Democrats organized House with help of other parties. (2) Democrats organized House because of Republican deaths. (3) Republican Sen. Jim Jeffords changed his party designation to Independent on June 5, 2001, switching control of the Senate to Democrats from Republicans. (4) Based on election returns of Nov. 5, 2002; figures may change because of absentee ballots and recounts. SOURCE: *The World Almanac and Books of Facts 2002 and news reports*

FLOOR LEADERS IN THE U.S. SENATE SINCE THE 1920S

Majority Leaders

Name	Party	State	Time in Office
Charles Curtis[1]	R	KS	1925-1929
James E. Watson	R	IN	1929-1933
Joseph T. Robinson	D	AR	1933-1937
Alben W. Barkley	D	KY	1937-1947
Wallace H. White	R	ME	1947-1949
Scott W. Lucas	D	IL	1949-1951
Ernest W. McFarland	D	AZ	1951-1953
Robert A. Taft	R	OH	1953
William F. Knowland	R	CA	1953-1955
Lyndon B. Johnson	D	TX	1955-1961
Mike Mansfield	D	MT	1961-1977
Robert C. Byrd	D	WV	1977-1981
Howard H. Baker, Jr.	R	TN	1981-1985
Bob Dole	R	KS	1985-1987
Robert C. Byrd	D	WV	1987-1989
George J. Mitchell	D	ME	1989-1995
Bob Dole	R	KS	1995-1996
Trent Lott	R	MS	1996-2001
Tom Daschle	D	SD	2001-2003
Trent Lott[3]	R	MS	2003-

Minority Leaders

Name	Party	State	Time in Office
Oscar W. Underwood[2]	D	AL	1920-1923
Joseph T. Robinson	D	AR	1923-1933
Charles L. McNary	R	OR	1933-1944
Wallace H. White	R	ME	1944-1947
Alben W. Barkley	D	KY	1947-1949
Kenneth S. Wherry	R	NE	1949-1951
Henry Styles Bridges	R	NH	1951-1953
Lyndon B. Johnson	D	TX	1953-1955
William F. Knowland	R	CA	1955-1959
Everett M. Dirksen	R	IL	1959-1969
Hugh D. Scott	R	PA	1969-1977
Howard H. Baker, Jr.	R	TN	1977-1981
Robert C. Byrd	D	WV	1981-1987
Bob Dole	R	KS	1987-1995
Tom Daschle	D	SD	1995-2001
Trent Lott	R	MS	2001-2003
Tom Daschle[3]	D	SD	2003-

NOTES: (1) First Republican to be chosen as floor leader. (2) First Democrat to be chosen as floor leader. (3) Based on election returns of Nov. 5, 2002. *SOURCE: The World Almanac and Books of Facts 2002*

SPEAKERS OF THE HOUSE OF REPRESENTATIVES

Parties: A, American; D, Democratic; DR, Democratic-Republican; F, Federalist; R, Republican; W, Whig

Name	Party	State	Time in Office	Name	Party	State	Time in Office
Frederick Muhlenberg	F	PA	1789-1791	James G. Blaine	R	ME	1869-1875
Jonathan Trumbull	F	CT	1791-1793	Michael C. Kerr	D	IN	1875-1876
Frederick Muhlenberg	F	PA	1793-1795	Samuel J. Randall	D	PA	1876-1881
Jonathan Dayton	F	NJ	1795-1799	Joseph W. Keifer	R	OH	1881-1883
Theodore Sedgwick	F	MA	1799-1801	John G. Carlisle	D	KY	1883-1889
Nathaniel Macon	DR	NC	1801-1807	Thomas B. Reed	R	ME	1889-1891
Joseph B. Varnum	DR	MA	1807-1811	Charles F. Crisp	D	GA	1891-1895
Henry Clay	DR	KY	1811-1814	Thomas B. Reed	R	ME	1895-1899
Langdon Cheves	DR	SC	1814-1815	David B. Henderson	R	IA	1899-1903
Henry Clay	DR	KY	1815-1820	Joseph G. Cannon	R	IL	1903-1911
John W. Taylor	DR	NY	1820-1821	Champ Clark	D	MO	1911-1919
Philip P. Barbour	DR	VA	1821-1823	Frederick H. Gillett	R	MA	1919-1925
Henry Clay	DR	KY	1823-1825	Nicholas Longworth	R	OH	1925-1931
John W. Taylor	D	NY	1825-1827	John N. Garner	D	TX	1931-1933
Andrew Stevenson	D	VA	1827-1834	Henry T. Rainey	D	IL	1933-1935
John Bell	D	TN	1834-1835	Joseph W. Byrns	D	TN	1935-1936
James K. Polk	D	TN	1835-1839	William B. Bankhead	D	AL	1936-1940
Robert M. T. Hunter	D	VA	1839-1841	Sam Rayburn	D	TX	1940-1947
John White	W	KY	1841-1843	Joseph W. Martin, Jr.	R	MA	1947-1949
John W. Jones	D	VA	1843-1845	Sam Rayburn	D	TX	1949-1953
John W. Davis	D	IN	1845-1847	Joseph W. Martin, Jr.	R	MA	1953-1955
Robert C. Winthrop	W	MA	1847-1849	Sam Rayburn	D	TX	1955-1961
Howell Cobb	D	GA	1849-1851	John W. McCormack	D	MA	1962-1971
Linn Boyd	D	KY	1851-1855	Carl Albert	D	OK	1971-1977
Nathaniel P. Banks	A	MA	1856-1857	Thomas P. "Tip" O'Neill, Jr.	D	MA	1977-1987
James L. Orr	D	SC	1857-1859	James Wright	D	TX	1987-1989
William Pennington	R	NJ	1860-1861	Thomas S. Foley	D	WA	1989-1995
Galusha A. Grow	R	PA	1861-1863	Newt Gingrich	R	GA	1995-1999
Schuyler Colfax	R	IN	1863-1869	J. Dennis Hastert	R	IL	1999-
Theodore M. Pomeroy	R	NY	1869				

SOURCE: The World Almanac and Books of Facts 2002

TIME LINE

1789	The 1st U.S. Congress convenes, March 4, in Federal Hall, New York City.
1790	Congress moves to Philadelphia, December 6.
1800	Congress meets November 17 for the first time at the Capitol in Washington, D.C.
1814	British troops set fire to the Capitol, August 24; Congress does not meet there again until 1819.
1861–65	Civil War.
1868	Pres. Andrew Johnson is impeached by the House, February 24; he is tried by the Senate and cleared, May 26.
1870	Hiram Revels, the first black member of Congress, takes his seat in the Senate.
1913	The Seventeenth Amendment is ratified, April 8, requiring that U.S. senators be directly elected by the people.
1917	The first woman in Congress, Jeannette Rankin, takes her seat in the House.
1934	For the first time, a regular session of Congress begins January 3, as required by the Twentieth Amendment.
1954	Sen. Joseph McCarthy is condemned by the Senate, December 2.
1973	Senate Watergate Committee investigates wrongdoing by Pres. Richard Nixon and his aides. Congress passes the War Powers Act.
1979	The House begins live TV coverage on C-SPAN; the Senate follows suit in 1986.
1989	Jim Wright is forced to resign as speaker of the House because of a financial scandal.
1994	Led by Newt Gingrich, Republicans win control of the House for the first time in forty years.
1997	Gingrich is fined $300,000 for violating ethics rules but keeps his House speakership.
1998	Pres. Bill Clinton is impeached, December 19, for trying to cover up a sex scandal; he is cleared by the Senate eight weeks later.
2002	Congressional elections leave Republicans in control of the presidency and both houses of Congress for the first time in five decades.

GLOSSARY

amendment: a change to the original Constitution; also, a change to a bill.

bill: an idea for a new law that has been presented to Congress for approval.

Civil War: a war (1861–65) between northern and southern states that began when states in the South rebelled against the Union and formed the Confederacy.

constitution: a document that defines the basic laws and ideas of a government.

demagogues: people who gain power by appealing to prejudice, hatred, and fear.

executive branch: the part of the U.S. government headed by the president.

filibuster: in the Senate, a series of very long speeches designed to stop a bill from coming to a vote.

framers: a name for the group of political leaders who wrote the U.S. Constitution.

judicial branch: the part of the U.S. government that is led by the Supreme Court.

legislative branch: the part of the U.S. government that is led by Congress.

open seat: a seat in the House or Senate for which no incumbent is running.

party primary: an election in which a political party chooses its candidate to run in the general election.

president pro tempore: the senator who presides over the Senate when the U.S. vice president is not there.

ratified: approved by the states; said of the Constitution and its amendments.

reapportionment: the process of changing the House after a census to reflect shifts in population among the states.

redistricting: the process of redrawing congressional district lines after reapportionment.

scourge: a source of pain, damage, or destruction.

seniority system: in Congress, a system in which the longest-serving members chair the most important committees.

speaker of the House: the member of the majority party who presides over the House.

State of the Union: a speech given each year by the president to both houses of Congress, meeting jointly.

veto: rejection by the president of a bill passed by Congress.

whip: a House or Senate leader who has the job of trying to make sure that members of the same party vote the same way on important issues.

TO FIND OUT MORE

BOOKS

Barone, Michael, et al.
The Almanac of American Politics 2002.
Washington, D.C.: National Journal, 2001. A new edition has been published for each Congress since 1972.

Davidson, Roger H., and Walter J. Oleszek.
Congress and Its Members.
Washington, D.C.: CQ Press, 2001 (8th ed.).

Greenberg, Ellen.
The House and Senate Explained: The People's Guide to Congress.
New York: W. W. Norton, 1996.

Ritchie, Donald A.
The Young Oxford Companion to the Congress of the United States.
New York: Oxford University Press, 1993.

Tarr, David R., and Ann O'Connor, eds.
Congress A to Z.
Washington, D.C.: Congressional Quarterly Inc., 1999 (3rd ed.).

INTERNET SITES

Architect of the Capitol
http://www.aoc.gov/homepage.htm
Guide to Capitol art and architecture.

C-SPAN
http://www.c-span.org/
Cable television network that covers Congress.

Library of Congress
http://www.loc.gov/
The official web site of the Library of Congress. Includes a special section on American history for young people.

Opensecrets.org
http://www.opensecrets.org/
Shows where senators and representatives get their campaign funds.

THOMAS—U.S. Congress on the Internet
http://thomas.loc.gov/
Official guide to recent legislation.

United States House of Representatives
http://www.house.gov/
The official House web site.

United States Senate
http://www.senate.gov/
The official Senate web site.

INDEX

Page numbers in *italic* type refer to illustration captions.

INDEX (CONT.)